*To my mom, Tanya H. Russell (1938–2014), who with love, patience,
and a storyteller's voice, read many a picture book to me.
She was a voracious reader who always kept a book or newspaper with her.
And to my dad, Charlie Russell Jr. (1932–2013), an exuberant writer
and a jazz aficionado —K.R.-B.*

To my daughter Tiffani, may all of your sweet dreams come true —F.M.

Back cover: Melba Liston, quoted in Linda Dahl, *Stormy Weather: The Music and Lives of a Century of Jazzwomen*
(New York: Limelight Editions, 1984), p. 252.

LEE & LOW BOOKS INC., 95 Madison Avenue, New York, NY 10016 • leeandlow.com
Book design by Stephanie Bart-Horvath • Book production by The Kids at Our House
The text is set in Gill Sans • The illustrations are rendered in oil paint
Manufactured in the United States of America by Worzalla Publishing Company, February 2015
10 9 8 7 6 5 4 3
First Edition

Library of Congress Cataloging-in-Publication Data
Russell-Brown, Katheryn.
Little Melba and her big trombone / by Katheryn Russell-Brown ; illustrations by Frank Morrison. — First edition.
pages cm
Summary: "A biography of African American musician Melba Doretta Liston, a virtuoso musician who played the trombone and composed and arranged
music for many of the great jazz musicians of the twentieth century. Includes afterword, discography, and sources"—Provided by publisher.
ISBN 978-1-60060-898-8 (hardcover : alk. paper)
1. Liston, Melba—Juvenile literature. 2. Jazz musicians—United States—Biography—Juvenile literature. 3. African American jazz musicians—
Biography—Juvenile literature. [1. Liston, Melba. 2. Jazz musicians. 3. African American jazz musicians.] I. Morrison, Frank, illustrator. II. Title.
ML3930.L566R87 2014 • 788.9'3165092—dc23 • [B] • 2013033662

FSC
MIX
Paper from
responsible sources
FSC® C002589
www.fsc.org

LITTLE MELBA AND HER BIG TROMBONE

by KATHERYN RUSSELL-BROWN

illustrations by FRANK MORRISON

Lee & Low Books Inc. ♫ New York

SPREAD THE WORD! Little Melba Doretta Liston was something special.

The year she was born was 1926. The place was Kansas City, where you could reach out and feel the music. The avenues were lined with jazz clubs, street bands, and folks harmonizing on every corner. All the hot music makers made sure they had a gig in KC.

From as far back as her memory would go, Melba loved the sounds of music. Blues, jazz, and gospel rhythms danced in her head—

the *plink* of a guitar,

the *hummmm* of a bass,

the **thrum-thrum** of a drum,

the *ping-pang* of a piano,

the *tremble* of a sweet horn.

Notes stirred and rhythms bubbled all through Melba's home. She couldn't get enough. Music was always on her mind.

She daydreamed about beats and lyrics.

Music was on Melba's mind at night too, when she should have been fast asleep.

Melba loved to hum along with the radio. Sometimes the music sounded so good she cupped her ear to the Majestic and closed her eyes. She especially loved Fats Waller, with his growly voice and booming piano.

The player piano came alive when Melba's kinfolk stopped by. While Melba pedaled, her aunties danced around the room.

With all that music flying by, Melba wanted to create her own sounds. When she was seven years old, she decided to sign up for music class at school.

What instrument could I play? Melba wondered.

At the traveling music store, Melba eyed a long, funny-looking horn.

"That one!" she cried. "It's beautiful!"

"A trombone?" Momma Lucille frowned. "It's big, and you're a little girl."

"*P l e e e e e a s e,*" Melba begged.

Momma Lucille bought the shiny trombone on the spot. She couldn't say no to her only child. Melba beamed from ear to ear and squeezed her new friend.

That night on the porch, Melba listened to Grandpa John play his guitar. This time she had her own music maker.

Grandpa John showed Melba how to cradle the horn. She tried to push out the slide, but her arm was too short. She had to tilt her head sideways and *streeeeeetch* out her right arm.

Melba gave the horn a mighty blow.

HooOooOoNK!
HAAAAAAAHNNNNK!

It sounded bad, like a howling dog.

"I'm no good, Grandpa," Melba said, tearing up.

"If you can blow, you can play," Grandpa John said. "Now stand up straight and blow steady."

Melba stayed up real late and practiced until she could play a simple tune all by herself.

Even with her keen ear, teaching herself to play the trombone was no piece of cake. But Melba kept blowing her horn, getting better day by day. The cool brass of the horn felt swell on her fingers.

Before long, Melba and her horn were making magic. She was only eight when the local radio station invited her to play a solo. Momma Lucille and Grandpa John were so proud as they watched little Melba play her big trombone.

Hard times hit rock bottom in 1937. That's when Melba and her mother moved to Los Angeles. The long train ride took them five states west and worlds away from Kansas City.

Melba's new teachers discovered that she was as smart as a whip. Her test scores were so high, the principal skipped her up from sixth grade to eighth.

In high school Melba joined Alma Hightower's famous after-school music club. Melba quickly became the star player in the club's band, The Melodic Dots.

The other club members struggled to keep up with Melba. Jealous boys called her bad names. She tried not to care, but way down deep the names hurt. Melba used her horn to turn all those hurt feelings into soulful music.

Melba's talent kept growing. She began writing music too. Then in 1943, when she was seventeen, Melba was invited to tour the country with a new band led by trumpet player Gerald Wilson.

"Go meet the world," Momma Lucille said, and hugged Melba good-bye. "You have my blessing."

Melba could feel it in her bones—the jazz scene was calling her name!

Traveling with the band was a thrill. Each city, from Salt Lake to New York, was an eyeful of something new.

Melba became a master musician. She composed and arranged music, spinning rhythms, harmonies, and melodies into gorgeous songs. And when Melba played the trombone, her bold notes and one-of-a-kind sound mesmerized the crowd.

Still, Melba was lonely. She was the only woman in the band. Some of the men were cruel. Others acted as if she wasn't there. Melba let the music in her head keep her company.

Rough times came when Melba traveled down South with singer Billie Holiday and her band. Some white folks didn't show good manners toward folks with brown skin. Hotel rooms were hard to come by, and the band members often had to sleep on the bus. Restaurants didn't always want their business. In the clubs, audiences sometimes just sat and stared at the band, or didn't show up at all.

Discouraged, Melba almost walked away from her trombone for good.

But Melba's fans wouldn't let her quit!

By the 1950s, all the cool jazz musicians wanted some Melba magic: Dizzy Gillespie, Duke Ellington, Quincy Jones, and more. They wanted to be on the bandstand with Melba and her divine horn. They wanted to play Melba's music.

Melba and her music trotted around the globe, dazzling audiences and making headlines in Europe, the Middle East, and Asia. All her life, Melba kept composing and arranging music, kept making her trombone sing.

Spread the word! Melba Doretta Liston was something special.

AFTERWORD

MELBA DORETTA LISTON (1926–1999) was a multitalented jazz virtuoso. A true pioneer, she was one of the first women, of any race, to become a world-class trombone player, composer, and arranger.

A self-taught child prodigy, Liston began playing trombone at age seven. Her musical gifts were so extraordinary that one of her teachers in Los Angeles asked Liston's mother for permission to adopt the young musician. The teacher wanted to work with Liston and then send her to the finest music teachers available. Liston's mother did not let her daughter go.

In high school Liston joined Alma Hightower's after-school music club. Hightower, an African American music educator, taught her students black history through music, dance, and poetry. At age sixteen, Liston left Hightower's group to become a professional musician. Once she had her membership card from the Los Angeles Musician's Union, Liston began playing with Bardu Ali's pit band at the Lincoln Theatre. While there, she also started writing music. After the

© Chuck Stewart

Melba Liston playing with The Dizzy Gillespie Big Band, Randall's Island, New York City, 1956

International Sweethearts of Rhythm band performed at the theater, they asked Liston to join them. She worked briefly with the famous all-girl group but then returned to Ali's band. In 1943, Liston, only seventeen years old, was hired for trumpeter Gerald Wilson's new band for a cross-country tour. She stayed with the band for five years.

When Wilson's band broke up, Liston joined the band led by famed trumpet player Dizzy Gillespie. A year later, the group disbanded, and in 1949, Liston was invited to play with Billie Holiday's band as it toured the South. The tour did not go well. The farther south the band traveled, the smaller the audiences became. They did not appreciate the band's new bebop sound. The tour was cut short, and the musicians had to call home for money so they could return to Los Angeles.

Liston decided to take a break from performing on the road. For a few years, she worked as a secretary at the Los Angeles Board of Education. She also had some small roles in movies.

In 1956, Liston returned to music. Dizzy Gillespie asked her to join his band on a tour of the Middle East and Asia for the US State Department. Then Quincy Jones took a band on tour in Europe and invited Liston to come with them. In 1957, Liston met composer and pianist Randy Weston. They collaborated often for the next forty years. Liston was the arranger for ten albums with Weston.

In 1958, *Melba Liston and Her 'Bones* was released. This album was the only one Liston recorded as the lead musician.

In the 1960s, Melba Liston wrote arrangements and conducted recordings for many of the popular musicians and groups. "Len Sirrah," a composition Liston wrote, was one of her favorites. From 1973 to 1979, Liston lived in Jamaica and taught at the University of the West Indies. When she came back to the United States, she formed her own band. Liston had a stroke in 1985 that left her partially paralyzed, and she was forced to give up playing her beloved trombone. With the aid of a computer,

Melba Liston with band leader Quincy Jones, New York City, 1960

Liston continued to compose and arrange works through the 1990s.

Liston received many honors for her jazz musicianship. In 1987, the National Endowment for the Arts named Liston a Jazz Master, the highest honor the United States gives to a jazz artist. The first International Women's Brass Conference in 1993 honored Liston as a brass woman pioneer. In 1995, Liston was interviewed by the Smithsonian for its Jazz Oral History Program.

Melba Liston's collaborations are legendary. She played with the best, among them Dexter Gordon, Gerald Wilson, Dizzy Gillespie, Billie Holiday, and Quincy Jones. She composed and arranged music for Duke Ellington, Count Basie, Randy Weston, Tony Bennett, Eddie Fisher, Billy Eckstine, the Supremes, Dinah Washington, Aretha Franklin, Ray Charles, Bob Marley, Marvin Gaye, and more. Today Melba Liston's sounds are heard across the black musical diaspora, including jazz, rhythm and blues, and reggae.

SELECTED DISCOGRAPHY

MELBA LISTON AS ARRANGER

Blakey, Art. *Hold On, I'm Coming*. Limelight LP, 1967; Universal Japan audio CD, 2011.

Gillespie, Dizzy. *Birks Works*. Verve LP, 1958; Verve 2 audio CDs, 1995; Verve MP3 file, 1995.

Jackson, Milt. *Milt Jackson and Big Brass: For Someone I Love*. Riverside LP, 1963; Original Jazz Classics audio CD, 1989; Riverside/Fantasy MP3 file, 2007.

Jones, Elvin. *And Then Again*. Atlantic LP, 1965; WEA Japan audio CD, 2012; Jazz All Stars MP3 file, 2013.

Mingus, Charles. *The Complete Town Hall Concert*. United Artists LP, 1962; Blue Note audio CD, 1994; Blue Note MP3 file, 1994.

Weston, Randy. *Earth Birth*. Verve audio CD, 1997; Verve MP3 file, 2012.

————. *Little Niles*. United Artists LP, 1959; Jazz Track audio CD, 2009.

————. *The Spirits of Our Ancestors*. Verve 2 audio CDs, 1992; Verve MP3 file, 2003.

Jackson, Milt. *Big Bags*. Riverside LP, 1962, OJC audio CD, 1991; Fantasy MP3 file, 2007.

Jones, Quincy. *I Dig Dancers*. Mercury LP, 1960; UNI Jazz France audio CD, 2010; Fresh Sound MP3 file, 2013.

————. *Q Live in Paris Circa 1960*. Warner Brothers LP, 1960; Qwest/Warner Brothers audio CD, 1996; HIP-O MP3 file, 2012.

————. *The Birth of a Band*. Mercury LP, 1959; Essential Jazz audio CD 2010.

Scott, Shirley. *Roll 'Em: Shirley Scott Plays the Big Bands*. Impulse LP, 1966; Impulse audio CD, 1994; Impulse MP3 file, 2004.

Wilson, Gerald. *Big Band Modern*. Audio Lab LP, 1954; Jazz Factory Spain audio CD, 2006; Jazz Factory MP3 file, 2006.

MELBA LISTON AS BAND LEADER

Liston, Melba. *Melba Liston and Her 'Bones*. Metrojazz LP, 1958; Fresh Sound audio CD, 2010; Fresh Sound MP3 file, 2011.

MELBA LISTON AS TROMBONE PLAYER

Davis, Eddie "Lockjaw." *Trane Whistle*. Prestige LP, 1960; OJC audio CD, 1991; Prestige MP3 file, 2006.

Gillespie, Dizzy. *At Newport*. Verve LP, 1957; Verve audio CD, 2007; Verve MP3 file, 2007.

————. *Dizzy in Greece*. Verve LP, 1957; Universal/Verve audio CD, 2005; Hallmark MP3 file 2010.

————. *World Statesman*. Norgran LP, 1956; Universal/Verve audio CD, 2005.

Author's Sources

Books and Articles

Blackburn, Julia. "Melba Liston: Strangers Down South." In *With Billie: A New Look at the Unforgettable Lady Day*, 239–247. New York: Vintage Books, 2006.

Bryant, Clora. "Melba Liston: NEA Jazz Master (1987)." Smithsonian Jazz Oral History Program NEA Jazz Master interview, December 4–5, 1996. http://www.smithsonianjazz.org/oral_histories/pdf/Liston.pdf.

———, et al., eds. "Melba Liston." In *Central Avenue Sounds: Jazz in Los Angeles*, 255–260. Berkeley and Los Angeles, CA: University of California Press, 1998.

Dahl, Linda. "Melba Liston: Trombonist and Arranger." In *Stormy Weather: The Music and Lives of a Century of Jazzwomen*, 250–259. New York: Limelight Editions, 1984.

Kaplan, Erica. "Melba Liston: It's All From My Soul." *Antioch Review* 57, no. 3 (Summer 1999): 415–425.

Oliver, Myrna. "Melba Liston; Jazz Trombonist, Composer." *Los Angeles Times*, April 28, 1999, Obituary sec. http://articles.latimes.com/1999/apr/28/news/mn-31919.

Perry, Paul Wardell. "Melba Liston's Slide to Success." *New Crisis* 107, no. 2 (March–April 2000): 35.

Placksin, Sally. *American Women in Jazz: 1900 to the Present: Their Words, Lives, and Music*. New York: Putnam, 1982.

Watrous, Peter. "Melba Liston, 73, Trombonist and Prominent Jazz Arranger." *New York Times*, April 30, 1999, Arts sec., Obituary. http://www.nytimes.com/1999/04/30/arts/melba-liston-73-trombonist-and-prominent-jazz-arranger.html.

Weston, Randy, and Willard Jenkins. "Enter Melba Liston." In *African Rhythms: The Autobiography of Randy Weston*, 70–78. Durham, NC: Duke University Press, 2010.

"Whatever Happened to Melba Liston?" *Ebony* 32 (June 1977): 122.

Interviews and Radio Broadcasts

Bradfield, Geof, musician and musical historian of Melba Liston. E-mail correspondence with the author, December 2012.

Drayton, Leslie, bandleader and Melba Liston's friend. Phone interview with the author, February 15, 2010.

Howze, Margaret, producer. "Women in Jazz, Part 2." *Jazz Profiles* from NPR. http://www.npr.org/programs/jazzprofiles/archive/women_2.html.

Narita, Cobi, Melba Liston's friend and manager. Phone interview with the author, March 25, 2010.

Weston, Randy, jazz pianist and composer. Phone interview with the author, April 28, 2010.

Wilson, Nancy, narrator. "Melba Liston: Bones of an Arranger." NPR's Jazz Profiles, NPR Music, July 9, 2008. http://www.npr.org/2008/07/09/92349036/melba-liston-bones-of-an-arranger.

Websites

"Melba Liston (1926–1999)." Susan Fleet Archives. http://archives.susanfleet.com/documents/melba_liston.html.

"Melba Liston Research Collective." Columbia College Chicago *CBMR Digest* 25, no. 2 (Fall 2012). http://www.colum.edu/CBMR/digest/2012/fall/liston.php.

"Melba Liston Scores and Other Material." Columbia College Chicago, Center for Black Music Research. http://www.colum.edu/CBMR/library/archives/personal/Melba_Liston_scores_and_other_material.php.

Sitaraman, Nicole Williams. "Melba Liston: Trombone Treasure." The Girls in the Band. http://www.thegirlsintheband.com/about/musicians/melbaliston/.

"Unsung Women of Jazz #6—Melba Liston." Curt's Jazz Cafe. http://curtjazz.com/2011/09/24/unsung-women-of-jazz-6-melba-liston/.